ABOVE TAHOE AND RENO

EMERALD BAY WINTER. *(See Page 108 for text)*

(Opposite) EMERALD BAY SUMMER.

TABLE OF CONTENTS

Putting together a book like ABOVE TAHOE AND RENO can be enormously complex and requires the help of many friendly, even dedicated people. So, for their encouragement and expertise, I thank the following:

Robert Burger, John Goy, Linda Henry, Tina Hodge, David Gregory, Yolanda Fillipone, Patricia O'Grady, Myrick Land, Steve Lapkin, Janet Lerude, Richard and Sue Stout, and Sandra Vlautin.

To Pilots: Dick Davis, Joe Isaia, Don Osborne, Jack Walther and Tim Willis.

A special salute to Perry Di Loreto for his piloting and his geographic expertise.

For assistance in researching the historical aerial photography, acknowledgement is made to the Nevada Historical Society, Special Collections, University of Nevada, Reno, Library for pages 8, 32, 72, 76.

CAMERON AND COMPANY

543 Howard Street   San Francisco, California 94105 USA   415/777-5582

Library of Congress Catalog Number: 95-92422
ABOVE TAHOE AND RENO ISBN: 0-918684-51-X
© 1995 by Robert W. Cameron and Company, Inc. All rights reserved.

First Printing, 1995

Book design by
JANE OLAUG KRISTIANSEN

Color processing by The New Lab, San Francisco and BWC Chrome Lab, Miami, Florida
Cameras by Pentax   Typography by Minnowillo and What a Beautiful Setting, San Francisco
Color Separations and Printing in South Korea

ABOVE TAHOE AND RENO

BY ROBERT CAMERON

A New Collection of Historical and
Original Aerial Photographs

With Text by
Warren Lerude

CAMERON AND COMPANY, SAN FRANCISCO, CALIFORNIA

In August of 1861, Mark Twain came upon Lake Tahoe.

"We plodded on, two or three hours longer, and at last the Lake burst upon us—a noble sheet of blue water lifted six thousand three hundred feet above the level of the sea, and walled in by a rim of snow-clad mountain peaks that towered aloft full three thousand feet higher still!...As it lay there with the shadows of the mountains brilliantly photographed upon its still surface I thought it must surely be the fairest picture the whole earth affords."

The words of Mark Twain, then a Virginia City newspaperman, are a fitting prologue for the images that aerial photographer Robert W. Cameron has created on film for the readers of this book.

The first good views of Lake Tahoe's glacially-created waters were noted about 12,000 years earlier by predecessors of Washoe Indian tribes.

What a sight they saw!

The previous two to four million years of seismic faultings had raised the Sierra Nevada on the West and the Carson Range to the East and created a basin in between. A glacier filled the basin and the ice remained for centuries.

As the Pleistocene ice age warmed, the melt down created the "Big Water" or "Tahoe" as the Indians came to call the lake.

The first non-natives to see the lake—February 14, 1844—were Captain John C. Fremont and his guide Kit Carson. They were in the neighborhood searching for a new path to California. Settlers and tourists have been coming to America's largest Alpine lake ever since.

Cameron, in his 84th year, focused on *Above Tahoe and Reno* after successfully photographing and publishing city and seascape books ranging from *Above San Francisco* to *Above Paris, New York, London, Chicago, Washington D.C., Los Angeles, Hawaii, Seattle, Yosemite, San Diego* and, most recently, *Above Carmel, Monterey and Big Sur* and *Above Mackinac.*

Cameron took to the air in fixed-wing airplanes and jet helicopter to capture views that surely would have inspired Mark Twain to dig deeply into his adjective bag for more colorful prose. Cameron affixed his Pentax 6 x 7 mm camera to a steadying hand-held gyroscope and focused through open aircraft windows at the historic splendor of the serene mountain lake and the contrasting neon-blaze of Reno.

The reader is taken on a tour from the high-rise hotel casinos of Stateline on the Nevada side of the South Shore to the adjacent City of South Lake Tahoe in California. Cameron's photographs capture the low water drought and expansive beaches of 1994 summer and the dramatic replenishing record snow depths of 1995 winter. Archival photographs reveal how vast forests were cut down for timber. The timber was pulled by steam boats across the lake to Glenbrook on the East Shore. Then, the timber was transported by wagons and railroads to Virginia City. The deep

mines of the Comstock Lode had to be shored up and trees were sparse on the Virginia Range.

In contrast, thick forests sprout today from the water's edge and are protected from encroachment by developers. Environmentalists are quick to challenge any kind of growth on the shoreline of Lake Tahoe. They were motivated following the 1960s and 70s boom of hotels and casinos on the South Shore. Buoy fields and piers are under close regulatory observation. Authorities worry about the ecology of the lake which is increasingly seen as a national treasure.

Tahoe's clear water shifts from brilliant aqua and turquoise near shallow shores to the midnight blue of the lake's greatest depth, 1,645 feet. Cameron's photographs capture dazzling sunlight and moody cloud patterns that emerge on the surface of the 12 by 22-mile lake. He focuses on classic mahogany runabouts in the Tahoe Yacht Club Concours d'Elegance near Homewood, Sunnyside, Tahoe City and Carnelian Bay.

A handful of hikers and mountain bikers are aware of the presence of Marlette Lake about 2,000 feet above Tahoe's East Shore. Birds and pilots also know it is there. Cameron's photographs take the reader to this historic reservoir. Through ingenious flume and pipeline engineering, Marlette fed water 2,000 feet down the eastern side of the mountain near Carson City and up to Virginia City via the world's longest inverted syphon. Thus Sierra water helped Nevada survive—and thrive.

Reno is the modern hub of Northwestern Nevada and the eastern slope of the Sierra. Interstate 80 runs through the city and connects the West and East coasts of the United States. U.S. Highway 395 runs north from Reno to Oregon, Washington and Canada and south to San Diego in California. The Reno-Tahoe International Airport serves over 500,000 passengers a month on major airlines. National firms, attracted by "free port" tax incentives, have built sprawling warehouses in Reno and Sparks for distribution of goods to the markets of the West.

Reno became a crossroads in the mid-19th century as pioneers passed through the Truckee Meadows on their way to California. These included the Donner Party which became trapped in 1846 snows near Truckee and turned to cannibalism to sustain life.

The first significant development in Reno was a bridge built in 1857 across the Truckee River. The Central Pacific Railroad tunneled through the Sierra and came to Reno on its way to Utah where it connected with the Union Pacific and the East. The Virginia and Truckee Railroad linked Reno to Carson City and Comstock Lode mines.

By 1861, President Lincoln appointed a governor for the new Territory of Nevada which was carved out of the Territory of Utah. In 1864, Nevada joined the Union as a state and the wealth of Virginia City's mines helped supply the Union

Army in the final days of the Civil War.

Charles Crocker, one of the "Big Four" San Franciscans who built the Central Pacific Railroad, envisioned Reno as the eventual largest metropolis between California and Missouri. Crocker suggested naming the little town "Reno" in honor of his friend General Jesse Lee Reno who had been killed in the Civil War.

Through the decades, Reno thrived on making legal that which was illegal everywhere else—including divorce and big-time boxing. Gambling was seen as sinful and banned in more polite societies so Nevada legalized it for economic advantage in 1931. Gambling and bootleg whiskey had flourished behind closed peephole doors of the Roaring 20s. Baby Face Nelson, Pretty Boy Floyd and, some say, even John Dillinger stopped by Reno while on the lam from midwestern crime sprees.

Famous authors also came to Reno. Sherwood Anderson wrote, in April, 1924:

"Everyone speaks of Reno and everyone has something different to say about it. It is one of the places in America. Larger cities, Detroit, Cincinnati, St. Louis and even that huge Chicago in some way get lost. One forgets just what is made in them—is it Fords or shoes or sealing wax? There are other towns about which folklore grows—Boston, New York, Baltimore, San Francisco, New Orleans, Reno. I fancy it because all of these have been the scene of real human adventures. Reno is the center, the metropolis of Nevada, and Nevada is something, and perhaps always will be something special."

Barbara and Myrick Land report in their new book *A Short History of Reno* that Mayor E.E. Roberts summed things up in his 1931 re-election bid:

"You cannot legislate morals into people, any more than you can legislate love into the hearts of some professed Christians. You can't stop gambling, so let's put it out in the open. Divorce is the only solution when marriages are unhappy. And if I had my way in this Prohibition year, I as mayor of Reno would place a barrel of whiskey on every corner, with a dipper, and a sign saying: 'Help yourself, but don't be a hog'."

For decades, Reno had a corner on the national gambling market. Reno was known world-wide, partly because of the promotional genius of "Pappy" Smith of Harolds Club and his advertising man Tom Wilson. They put up "Harolds Club or Bust" signs from the Antarctic to Guam to New York.

The "Biggest Little City in the World" took on new sophistication in the 1960s and 70s as Bill Harrah set the style with the likes of Sinatra, Judy Garland, Cosby, Sammy Davis, Jr., Barbra Streisand and John Denver. But Reno lost its national luster in the 1980s and dwindled as a regional gambling center for San Francisco and Pacific Northwest tourists.

Then, in the 1990s, gambling was legalized across America forcing Reno into a crossroad. The challenge was psychological and economic. Should Reno try to compete in the new major leagues of Las Vegas and national gaming and tourism?

The entrepreneurial answer was yes. And in 1994 and 1995 the boom went wild when Reno attorney Don Carano put together a team to build Nevada's tallest hotel-casino, the 37-story Silver Legacy. The spirit caught on and the other hotels expanded for a bold, new day. The new National Bowling Stadium was created to attract 100,000 competitors a year.

Meantime, the flight of Californians from high taxes and soaring crime rates brought Reno thousands of new residents. They sought the high desert, Alpine lifestyle that Reno and Lake Tahoe provide in leafy-green summer, golden autumn, snow-filled winter and a spring-time of wildflowers and Sierra waterfalls.

Many were drawn to the University of Nevada. The campus, with its picturesque, grassy quad and brick buildings, has been the location for many Hollywood movies. The university is home for academic disciplines as divergent as mining, agriculture, medicine, journalism, business, music and Basque studies. The National Judicial College attracts judges from around the world.

Almost everyone seems to be having a good time. Especially those who golf from March to December, sail from May Day to Halloween and ski on up to 65 feet of Sierra snowfall from Thanksgiving until the Fourth of July.

Reno and Lake Tahoe. A city on the edge of a desert. A lake as picturesque as the Swiss Alps. Reno and Tahoe are as different as night and day. Yet they are bound together by lifestyle choice, entrepreneurial grit and a sense of adventure as Robert Cameron's photographs so eloquently show in this book.

—*Warren Lerude*

ROBERT CAMERON   WARREN LERUDE

LAKE TAHOE IN SUMMER AND AUTUMN

STATELINE. Harvey Gross set the high-rise gambling pace on the South Shore in 1961 with his Wagon Wheel. Visitors now flock to 10,000 rooms in Nevada hotel-casinos and adjacent California motels.

Edgewood Tahoe Golf Course stretches 7,491 yards through pines and meadows next to U.S. Highway 50 in Nevada. Par is 72 for 18 holes.

STATELINE. Nevada Beach at the base of Round Hill links with beaches of
Stateline and California's City of South Lake Tahoe. Autumn snowfall near
Heavenly Valley whets skiers' appetite.

Paddle wheeler Tahoe Queen survives decade of drought by remaining
afloat in sandy waters at Ski Run Marina in the summer of 1994.

TAHOE KEYS. A narrow channel enables motor craft and sailboats to ease through shallow water to marina and luxury home slips. Evaporation lifts 1,400,000 tons of water a day from the 12 by 22-mile lake. The surface covers 191.6 square miles. Tahoe's record high was 6,231.26 feet above sea level in July, 1907. The record low was 6,220.26 feet in November, 1992.

SOUTHWEST SHORE. Tahoe colors shift from transparent water lapping at beaches to aqua coves and midnight blue depths. Water temperatures range from 68 to 39 degrees. The deepest point is 1,645 feet and is about four and one half miles south of Kings Beach off the North Shore. The lake is so clear a rock the size of a dinner plate is visible at 75 feet.

(Opposite) FALLEN LEAF LAKE. Washoe Indians called the lake Doolaga (Fallen Leaf) because they believed the Good Spirit changed leaves to water. E.B. Scott tells the story in *The Saga of Lake Tahoe.* Stanford University alumni gather at their own camp near the marina on the West Shore. The 418-foot-deep lake is 90 feet above Lake Tahoe. Hollywood's "The Bodyguard" was filmed here.

MEEK'S BAY. Washoe Indians camped near these white, sandy beaches. In the 1860s, vast forests were felled. Logs were towed across the lake by steam tugs to Glenbrook for use as timber in Virginia City's mines. Naturalist John Muir called trees of nearby Sugar Pine Point "priests of the forest extending their arms in benediction over the congregation."

HOMEWOOD. Sixty-five vintage "Tahoe Woodies" parade in Tahoe Yacht Club Concours d'Elegance off Homewood and Obexer's West Shore marinas. Observes: Concours Chairman Steven A. Lapkin: "The Smithsonian would likely consider it 'The most authentic and diversified public presentation of privately-owned wooden run-abouts in the United States'."

The first Gar Woods came to Obexer's in 1928. Other Tahoe classics are Chris-Craft and Hacker Craft, Century and Barnes.

FLEUR DU LAC. "Location. Location. Location," as they say in real estate. Industrialist Henry J. Kaiser built his estate on Homewood Bay near Blackwood Canyon in 1939. The main house included built-in water garages for speed boats, a breakwater and a light house. The wedding scene in "The Godfather" was filmed at Fleur du Lac. It is now an enclave of expensive homes.

SUNNYSIDE. Sugar pines of Ward Creek Canyon were turned into railroad ties in 1866 and floated from Tahoe City on the Truckee River to Coburn's Station, now Truckee. The ties became the bed for the emerging Central Pacific Railroad. Sunnyside has served as "headquarters" for San Franciscans in search of lakeside sun, boating and dining.

(Opposite) TAHOE CITY. The Truckee River begins at Tahoe City as Lake Tahoe reaches its natural rim of 6,223 feet above sea level and the water spills through the gates at the Fanny Bridge dam. The dam can hold back another six feet, one inch of water in abundant snow years. Tahoe City includes several shopping centers and a major marina.

(Opposite) CARNELIAN BAY. Sierra Boat Co. marina houses vintage wooden speed-boats and modern craft at Carnelian Bay. This was one of many communities served in the 19th century by steamboats. Eventually, dirt roads were carved out of the wilderness and then modernized around the 71-mile shoreline.

KINGS BEACH. Bing began the forerunner of the famous "Crosby" at Brockway Golf Course while entertaining at nearby Cal-Neva Lodge. Marshy conditions limited the original course to 12 holes in 1924. Eventually, it was scaled to the current nine holes, 3,237 yards. Par is 36. Kings Beach is known for its wide beaches and shallow wading water.

BROCKWAY AND CRYSTAL BAY. Brockway's Hot Springs Hotel welcomed turn-of-century visitors to a rustic California setting. Nevada's slot machines clang near Crystal Bay's quiet beaches. In 1927, the hotel Cal-Neva straddled the state line. Rumors spread in the 1930s that gangsters "Baby Face" Nelson and "Pretty Boy" Floyd were hanging around. In the 1950s and 60s, the Cal-Neva made news as a playground for Frank Sinatra and other Hollywood stars.

(Opposite) INCLINE AND THE NEVADA SHORE. Devastating forest fire smoke rises northwest to Mt. Rose above tranquil Incline. Sand Harbor is part of the 14,000-acre Lake Tahoe Nevada State Park. The property was once owned by a San Francisco real estate baron, "Captain" George Whittell.

INCLINE. The Robert Trent Jones Golf Course stretches 6,910 yards over 18 holes with par of 72. Million-dollar homes line fairways in the pines. The Hyatt Hotel and Casino complex reaches to sandy beaches. Incline's population has grown to 7,500. Many residents wish to break away from Washoe County and Reno and form an independent county.

MARLETTE LAKE. An earthen dam was built 2,000 feet above the east shore of Lake Tahoe to create Marlette Lake in 1876. Water was transported via a 32-mile network of flumes and pipelines including 4,000 feet of tunnel blasted through granite. The dam water raced down the world's longest inverted syphon toward Carson City. Pressure drove the water across the valley and up another mountain to Virginia City where it cooled the mines and mixed with the abundant whiskey supply. The system delivered 6,600,000 gallons every 24 hours. Marlette still serves Virginia and Carson cities today.

(Opposite) GLENBROOK. This scenic and historic settlement is a retreat today for wealthy San Franciscans and others from around the world. Author Sessions S. Wheeler tells in *Tahoe Heritage* how the timber-wealthy Bliss family built a summer home at Glenbrook in 1872. Their Lake Tahoe Railway and Transportation Company hauled logs to sawmills at Spooner Summit. The family built the fashionable Glenbrook Inn. Celebrity guests ranged through the decades from Ulysses S. Grant to Bret Harte, Thomas Edison, Clark Gable and Rita Hayworth.

CAVEROCK. In the 1860s, mule teams and freight wagons skirted the watery edge on a narrow bridge of timber. E.B. Scott's *The Saga of Lake Tahoe* tells tales of Paiutes and Washoe Indians fighting battles at the dramatic site for control of "Big Water" Tahoe. The first traffic tunnel was blasted open in 1931, the second in 1957.

SPOONER SUMMIT. The heavily traveled summit links South Lake Tahoe and Carson City. The forests are now protected from the kind of logging operations that devastated the area in the 1870s to provide timber for Virginia City's mines.

KINGSBURY GRADE. Housing projects sprawl today at the top of Kingsbury Grade. The twisting mountain road joins Carson Valley with Heavenly Valley Ski Resort and Stateline casinos. On April 28, 1860, the Pony Express inaugurated its Kingsbury run from Friday's Station near Stateline to Van Sickle's Station near Genoa.

Four years earlier, Norwegian emigrant John A. "Snowshoe" Thompson skied through the mountain pass carrying mail from the Carson Valley to Placerville 90 miles west. Thompson helped pioneer Sierra long-board skiing on his 10-foot, 25-pound skis.

Lake Tahoe's Ski Resorts

MARK TWAIN'S TAHOE. "A noble sheet of blue water lifted six thousand three hundred feet above the level of the sea, and walled in by a rim of snow-clad mountain peaks that towered aloft full three thousand feet higher still!... I thought it must surely be the fairest picture the whole earth affords." So wrote Mark Twain who first saw Lake Tahoe in August, 1861.

Today, the 30 runs of 8,540-foot Diamond Peak Ski Resort afford spectacular views of the lake. Seven lifts serve 655 skiable acres with a vertical drop of 1,840 feet.

(Opposite) NORTHSTAR-AT-TAHOE. Nestled in the forest beneath the 8,610-foot Mt. Pluto, Northstar's 11 lifts serve 60 runs and 2,000 alpine acres. The vertical drop is 2,200 feet. Another 65 kilometers stretch over 38 nordic trails. Vacation homes line an 18-hole golf course in the pines.

INTERSTATE 80 AT BOREAL.
A statue of Snowshoe Thompson stands outside the Auburn Ski Club's Western Wintersport Museum near Donner Summit. Exhibits feature long-board ski racing by pioneers in the 1860s. Boreal is usually the first of Tahoe ski areas to open. Its 41 runs and 7,800-foot peaks are served by nine lifts. A sister resort, Soda Springs, includes and 16 runs.

DONNER LAKE AND MEMORIAL.
A statue memorializing Donner Party pioneers trapped in 1846 storms is located at the California State Park Emigrant Trail Museum. The 22-foot pedestal marks the depth of the snow that winter. The pioneers arrived at Donner Lake October 31. Many resorted to cannibalism to avoid starvation. Forty-two men, women and children died and 49 survived in makeshift camps. Some were not rescued until April of 1847.

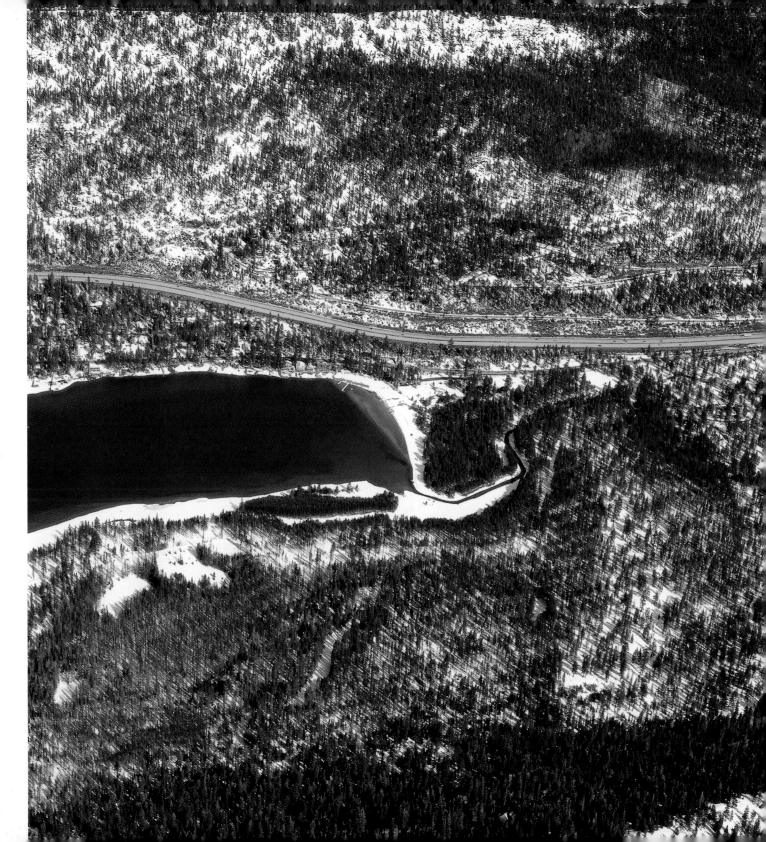

ROYAL GORGE. Eighty-eight ski trails, including these in Van Norden Meadows, wind 185 miles to make Royal Gorge the world's largest privately owned nordic ski area. The 9,172-acre resort is 7,000 feet above sea level. It uses four surface lifts to elevate skiers to different levels of runs, 12 warming huts and four trail-side cafes. On a busy day, 2,300 skiers scamper over the hilly terrain. The main Royal Gorge lodge is just beyond the Soda Springs ski area at upper left.

(Opposite) SUGAR BOWL. Skiers park cars on old U.S. Highway 40 and ride a "Magic Carpet" gondola across the valley to the lodge and 8,383-foot Mt. Lincoln. The one-time enclave for wealthy San Franciscans has expanded to 1,110 acres of skiing with 1,500 feet of vertical drop. Fifty-eight runs are served by nine lifts. Mt. Disney is named for original investor Walt Disney whose early cartoons featured "Goofy" on skis.

(Overleaf) *SQUAW VALLEY U.S.A.* Thousands ski Squaw Valley USA on major holidays such as the President's Weekend in February. The 33 lifts serve 4,000 acres on six mountains. The vertical drop is 2,850 feet from Granite Chief at 9,050 feet. A slalom course stretches over lower portion of famed KT 22. This was the site of the women's downhill race in the 1960 Winter Olympic Games.

DONNER SUMMIT. Old U.S. Highway 40 dead-ends in snow but is open during the spring, summer and autumn. Legend has it that Soda Springs Olympic skier Dick Buek flew his light plane beneath Rainbow Bridge. He didn't. He was killed, however, when he crashed the plane in Donner Lake. At right, Donner Ski Ranch's six lifts serve 40 runs.

HIGH CAMP. The complex is located 2,000 feet above the parking lot. It includes an Olympic-size ice arena, heated swimming pools, a bungee tower, restaurants and ski school. At left is Siberia Bowl and 8,900-foot Squaw Peak. Some extreme skiers dash between huge rocks into ski movie stardom. Others careen into obscurity.

SQUAW VALLEY USA. Skiers scramble off the Siberia Express lift near Squaw Peak high above Lake Tahoe. The men's Olympic downhill started here. This above tree-line skiing is similar to terrain in Europe's Alps. Founder Alex Cushing designates the entire area skiable and does not name most individual runs.

Instead, he identifies lifts and peaks. Below left are Gold Coast restaurants and gondola. At left of Siberia Bowl is the top of the lift serving the notoriously steep Headwall.

At right of the parking lot are KT 22, Olympic Lady and Red Dog. They link with the Snow King peak. The Resort at Squaw Creek's Robert Trent Jones Jr. 18-hole golf course is buried under snow.

(Opposite) *ALPINE MEADOWS*. More than 100 runs are served by 12 lifts and spread over 2,080 acres at Alpine Meadows. The vertical drop is 1,802 feet from 8,637-foot Ward Peak. The main lodge area includes Scott Peak and Alpine Bowl with sweeping views of Lake Tahoe. The vast Sherwood bowls are on the south side of the mountain.

SKI HOMEWOOD. On the West Shore of Lake Tahoe skiers ride nine lifts for a vertical rise of 1,650 feet at Homewood. They ski over 1,260 acres on 57 runs. Ski Homewood sits so close to Lake Tahoe skiers feel they can dive from snow to water. The runs are tucked away in the forest beyond California State Route 89 and can best be identified from an aerial perch such as this.

HEAVENLY SKI RESORT. The face is the first dramatic introduction for skiers riding a tram from the 6,540-foot base. The 4,800-acre resort straddles the stateline. Skiers command dramatic views of Lake Tahoe from the California side. On the Nevada side, skiers take long runs off 10,040-foot peaks. Twenty-four lifts serve 79 runs. Stateline, Nevada, hotel casinos are minutes away from either the California or Nevada bases of Heavenly Valley.

KIRKWOOD. This resort is a remote 35 miles southwest of South Lake Tahoe on California State Route 88. Skiers climb from Kirkwood Meadows to Thimble Peak at 9,876 feet. Eleven lifts serve 2,300 acres including a 2.5-mile run. Nordic skiers find 48 miles of track. Plans call for a ski resort village and lift expansion including snow-making equipment

(Above and Opposite) MT. ROSE SKI AREA. Lifts rise 1,400 feet up Northwest Passage from the main lodge to the 9,700-foot Slide Mountain. The resort is just across Nevada State Route 431 from the 10,776-foot Mount Rose. Five lifts serve 41 runs spread over 900 acres. At the top of the Northwest lift, skiers cross to the East Bowl which offers views of Nevada's mountain and desert terrain.

SKI MOUNTAINS IN SUMMER. The winding Mt. Rose Highway *(opposite)* leads to a side road serving the East Bowl of Slide Mountain. Hang gliders launch here and sail over Washoe Valley. A three-hour trek leads to the Mount Rose summit's clear air above Lake Tahoe. Wrote Mark Twain in *Roughing It:* "The air up there in the clouds is very pure and fine, bracing and delicious. And why shouldn't it be ?—it is the same the angels breathe."

Skiers turned summer-time hikers come back to many areas such as Alpine Meadows, above, and trek from meadows to peaks.

SQUAW VALLEY IN SUMMER. Visitors from around the world are attracted to the site of the 1960 Winter Olympic Games for summer recreation. This includes hiking, swimming, horseback riding, mountain biking and play on the Robert Trent Jones Jr. 18-hole championship golf course.

Skaters whirl beneath a canopy that protects the ice from sunshine. A World Cup-size soccer field hosts training camps and competition. Concerts are staged beneath the stars.

TRUCKEE AND THE HIGH COUNTRY

TRUCKEE AND DONNER LAKE. This historic community of boutiques and restaurants is the heart of the Tahoe/Donner residential area.

Truckee was named for a Paiute Indian guide who helped emigrants cross the Sierra in 1844. The incorporated area population is 9,985 and the town draws from 30,000 people who live in nearby mountains and valleys.

(Opposite) DONNER LAKE. Three miles long and three quarters of a mile wide, was named for the Donner Party trapped in deep snows of 1846. *(See Page 39 for detail.)*

DONNER SUMMIT. Climbers scale granite cliffs on old U.S. Highway 40 near the Donner Ski Ranch. Neighboring Alpine Skills International is a mountaineering center. The present-day railroad is south of an original abandoned tunnel. Interstate 80 relieved motorists of treacherous winter driving on Highway 40.

(Opposite) GRAEAGLE. The Feather River skirts the Plumas Pines Golf Resort and Di Loreto home development at Graeagle. 72, 18-hole, 6,504-yard course is one of several at Graeagle. The population expands to about 3,000 during the summer. Graeagle is 45 miles north of Truckee on California State Route 89.

PORTOLA. Railroads have used Portola as a terminal center since the first freight train passed through in 1909. The Feather River rail route begins in Oakland and continues east toward Nevada.

LAKE DAVIS. Fly fishing yields two and three-pound fighting rainbow trout. Drought-stricken beaches disappear under rising spring-time waters in heavy snow years. Lake Davis is about seven miles north of Portola.

BOCA DAM AND RESERVOIR. This is one of several California reservoirs north of Interstate 80 that provide storage for downstream Nevada communities, agriculture and the Pyramid Lake Indian Reservation. A 10-year drought drained the reservoirs dry. They were replenished by the melting snow of the 1995 record winter.

FEATHER RIVER CANYON. A Union Pacific train snakes past a trestle in the Feather River Canyon on its way from Quincy past Graeagle to Portola and points east.

(Opposite) TRUCKEE RIVER CANYON. Southern Pacific tracks parallel Interstate 80 and the wooden power flume in the Truckee River Canyon between Truckee and Reno.

RENO

R FOR RENO. A white-washed "R" is painted in the rocky sagebrush hills north of Reno. This is a tradition in Nevada cities and towns. A nearby hill *(opposite)* has an "N" for Nevada.

The National Basque Monument pays homage to sheepherders. The 26-foot bronze was sculpted by Nestor Basterretxea of San Sebastian, Spain. He commemorated "A man solitary and strong, held straight by his own will, patient laborer facing onto the uncertain horizon of adventure." Carmelo Urza tells the story in his book *SOLITUDE*.

(Opposite) *FOREST FIRE ABOVE RENO.* Hundreds of thousands of timbered acres burn in Sierra forests around Reno and Lake Tahoe during hot, dry summers. Firefighters worked around the clock to control this fire in the hills of Verdi west of Reno. The blaze threatened homes and casinos near Interstate 80. Reno's Moana Lane and Washoe County Golf Course are in foreground.

BOOMTOWN. Truck drivers pace themselves across Western America to stop for diesel fuel and relaxation at the Boomtown Hotel and Casino west of Reno at Verdi. Nearly 700 trucks have been parked at the 640-acre complex at one time. Drivers often wait out snowstorms that close Interstate 80. The resort includes a non-gaming, family entertainment center for the "under 21" crowd.

HISTORIC RENO CENTER. Virginia Street and the Truckee River are the historic heart of Reno. A new "Riverwalk" celebrates the mountain stream's flow through the city. The first bridge was built in 1857. Landmark Riverside and Mapes hotels were closed and by-passed as the gaming center moved north of the river.

Celebrities in search of divorce were attracted to another landmark, the Washoe County Court House. Columnist Walter Winchell tabbed them "Reno-vated". Legend has it divorcees tossed their diamond rings into the Truckee River.

(Opposite) *THE NEW RENO.* Nevada's tallest hotel-casino, the Silver Legacy, rises 37 stories as the centerpiece of the newly developed downtown Reno. The Silver Legacy ties together the Eldorado Hotel and Casino and Circus Circus. Combined, they total 4,160 rooms, 6,000 slot machines and 290 table games. The National Bowling Stadium attracts over 100,000 competitors in a tournament year.

MANSIONS ON THE TRUCKEE. The great old houses of early 20th Century Reno range in architecture from Colonial white to red brick Tudor and earth-tone Mediterranean stucco. The largest of the private homes was built in the style of an Italian villa in 1906 by Senator George Stuart Nixon. It has been restored and subsequently ravished by fire.

UNIVERSITY OF NEVADA. The landmark Morrill Hall was built in 1885 when the 11-year-old university moved from Elko to Reno. Several historic buildings remain on the campus. The grassy, tree-lined "quad" was designed in 1906 to emulate Thomas Jefferson's "academical village" at the University of Virginia. The President's House, lower right, was torn down in 1957 to make way for new buildings. The old Mackay Stadium site is now occupied by the Ansari Business Building, the Reynolds School of Journalism and other buildings. The stadium and other sports facilities are now on the northern rim of the campus.

SUBURBAN RENO. The "Biggest Little City in the World" has been known for decades of casino gambling. Downtown Reno continues to burst with new hotels and casinos. Suburban Reno is filled with parks and lakes. and walkers circle Virginia Lake, in photograph at left. Migrating Canadian geese stop by for a cruise. The Robert Trent Jones 71-par, 18-hole golf course stretches 6,703 yards around expensive Lakeridge homes.

GOLFBALLS... The 18-hole, 72-par Rosewood Lakes Municipal Golf Course weaves 6,700 yards through natural wetlands. The water attracts geese, ducks, pelicans and doves. In the photograph at right is the private Hidden Valley Country Club.

... AND COYOTES. Hidden Valley Country Club is Reno's longest course at 7,061 yards. Par is 72 for 18 holes. The wetlands attract thirsting wild horses called mustangs. Coyotes scamper out of sagebrush and lope across fairways to ponds. Residents lock up cats and small dogs at night lest they become a coyote's supper.

SAGEBRUSH SPRAWL. Once upon a time, they came to Reno to gamble, get a divorce or escape high taxes. Some simply liked high desert air. They're still coming. New residents are building homes where sagebrush once grew. The photograph above is Di Loreto Sierra Highlands community of 800 homes and 30-acre shopping center. Opposite is part of the huge Caughlin Ranch development.

Author Robert Laxalt wrote in *Nevada A Bicentennial History:* "I find myself reflecting whimsically on how very much like the sagebrush the people are, at least in the hinterland that makes up most of Nevada, setting down their roots and thriving in unlikely places, hardy and resilient, stubborn and independent, restrained by environment and yet able to grow free."

RENO. Downtown comes alive as 1950s-style cars parade beneath the world-famous Reno Arch in "Hot August Nights" celebration. Reno, once the gambling capital of the country, now stays competitive as a special events center with rodeos, balloon and high-speed air races and new casinos and hotel towers.

NO SAND TRAP? But there's plenty of water hazard at the Reno Hilton's driving range *(opposite)*. The 2,001-room hotel anchors "greens" 200 feet off the concrete shore. Floating golf balls are plucked by boat and butterfly net from the 40-acre, 167-foot-deep lake.

The expanding 1,078-room Peppermill and 587-room Clarion hotels are south of downtown. The 500,000-square-foot convention center hosts family activities as well as business meetings. Reno's colorful past has been documented in many books including *A Short History of Reno* by authors Barbara and Myrick Land.

RENO AIR RACES. The National Championship Air Races draw l50,000 visitors to the Reno/Stead Airport north of the city. Pilots of 450 private planes have parked at Jet West next to the Reno-Tahoe International Airport.

P-38 pilot Lefty Gardner *(opposite)* rounds a pylon at 400 miles an hour. He leads P-51 Mustangs, Grumman Bearcats and other World War II fighter planes in the unlimited race. Legend has it he flys so low his wing clips the sagebrush.

RENO AND ITS NEIGHBORS

SPARKS. John Ascuaga's Nugget dominates Victorian Square center of Sparks. Ascuaga, the son of a Basque sheepherder, developed the Nugget into 84,000 square feet of gaming with 1,200 slot machines and 1,000 hotel rooms. The Nugget is famous for pet elephant Bertha who inaugurated the Circus Room in 1962 when she was 12. She continues to perform twice nightly.

Sparks is a railroad terminal city immediately east of Reno. It also serves as a national distribution center. Free port status provides tax incentives for firms storing merchandise in the huge warehouses.

(Opposite) MUSTANGS. Nevada is home to 26,700 wild horses and burros. The U.S. Bureau of Land Management maintains this center in Palomino Valley where 1,800 animals can be cared for at one time. When certified healthy, they are put up for adoption. Nearly 10,000 are sent across the nation to adopters each year. Fee for a horse is $125, a burro, $75.

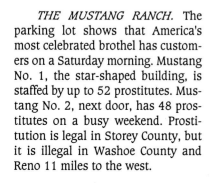

THE MUSTANG RANCH. The parking lot shows that America's most celebrated brothel has customers on a Saturday morning. Mustang No. 1, the star-shaped building, is staffed by up to 52 prostitutes. Mustang No. 2, next door, has 48 prostitutes on a busy weekend. Prostitution is legal in Storey County, but it is illegal in Washoe County and Reno 11 miles to the west.

PYRAMID LAKE. The 23 by 10 mile lake is what's left of prehistoric Lake Lahontan. Author Sessions S. Wheeler's classic *The Desert Lake* explains its formation 70,000 years ago as glaciers carved much of North America. Cavemen looked upon its waters 11,000 years ago. Today, the Pyramid Lake Paiute Indian Reservation oversees fishing for the four-pound cut-throat trout. The prehistoric cui-ui (quee-wee) is an endangered species known only to these waters.

(Overleaf) The Pyramid-shaped rock stands 90 feet above the water. Anaho Island is a government-protected pelican reserve. The lake is 36 miles northeast of Reno.

97

(*Opposite*) *VIRGINIA CITY.* Virginia City. Silver miners struck it rich in the 1859 discovery of the Comstock Lode. The mines eventually yielded $400,000,000 in silver and gold. Young Samuel Clemens showed up in 1861, took the pen name Mark Twain and began his literary career as a reporter for the *Territorial Enterprise*. Virginia City millionaires built mansions, churches and an opera house. The city of 30,000 claimed the West's first steam elevator. Actress Sarah Bernhardt came to town. So did President U.S. Grant. Comstock Lode millionaires helped build San Francisco.

BOWERS' MANSION. Eilley Orrum and Sandy Bowers married in 1859 and pooled their mining claims. They built a mansion in Washoe Valley and hosted elegant parties. Sandy died in 1868 and Eilley's fortune declined rapidly. She turned to fortune telling in Virginia City and died in poverty. Their graves are on a hill behind the mansion. The mansion and grounds are now part of a Washoe County Park.

WASHOE LAKE. Drought-stricken Washoe Lake between Reno and Carson City is replenished by melting Sierra Nevada snows. When the water is up, this is a favorite spot for wind-surfers because of stiff breezes that flow from Slide Mountain.

(Opposite) NEVADA'S CAPITAL. Carson City's principal government buildings are the Nevada Legislature, Supreme Court and Capitol, from left. The Nevada State Museum is located in the old U.S. Mint where the famed "CC" Carson City dollars were made from Comstock Lode silver.

THE GOVERNOR'S MANSION. It is located in a tree-lined neighborhood of Victorian homes. Carson City was named for frontier guide Kit Carson. Established in 1858, it became the capital following statehood in 1864 and has grown to a population of about 40,000.

NEVADA STATE PRISON. The old Nevada State Prison had a casino for inmates. The warden reckoned gambling was legal in Nevada, so why restrict it here? Eventually, the casino was closed. At right, the new prison has a less ominous "yard". Both are in Carson City.

CARSON VALLEY. Explorers moved through this fertile country in the 1840s. Ranchers followed and settled. Modern-day emigrants are filling the valley from hills on the north near Carson City to the main communities of Minden and Gardnerville. Basque restaurants attract locals and tourists alike. Growth includes high tech industry, housing developments and golf courses.

(Opposite) GENOA. Mormon Station became the first settlement of Nevada in 1851. The name was changed to Genoa in 1856 to honor Columbus' birthplace. Traders served pioneers moving through mountain passes to California. Today, the town of Genoa has a population of 200 and another 500 live close by. A "candy dance" is held in the autumn to raise money for civic improvements. People come from miles around.

THE SERENITY OF TAHOE. (Cover) Snowy peaks ring America's largest alpine lake in this fish-eye photograph made by Robert Cameron from a helicopter above the historic North Shore. Nevada's East Shore is on the left, California's West Shore on the right and the Stateline casino area on the 22-mile distant South Shore.

THE GLITTER OF RENO. (Back Cover) The 37-story Silver Legacy is the center-piece of the new Reno downtown center which includes the National Bowling Stadium. The Truckee River is the historic heart of Reno. This photograph was made by Robert Cameron at dusk as neon glowed to greet the coming evening.

EMERALD BAY. (Photographs on pages 2 and 3) Lake Tahoe and Emerald Bay do not freeze but fierce winter storms bring ice to neighboring Cascade Lake. Crystal clear waterfalls and streams flow to Lake Tahoe each spring. Hollywood filmed "Rose Marie" at Cascade Lake in 1935, "A Place in the Sun" in 1949.

Emerald Bay's island served as a tea house for Vikingsholm. Laura Moore Knight built the replica of an ancient Viking castle in 1929 on the West Shore. It is now a California State Park.

OTHER BOOKS BY ROBERT CAMERON: *Hardcover, one hundred sixty full color pages, 11 x 14 inches.*

ABOVE SEATTLE with Emmett Watson
ABOVE CHICAGO with Tim Samuelson and Cheryl Kent
ABOVE SAN FRANCISCO with Herb Caen
ABOVE LOS ANGELES with Jack Smith
ABOVE SAN DIEGO with Neil Morgan
ABOVE YOSEMITE with Harold Gilliam
ABOVE LONDON with Alistair Cooke
ABOVE PARIS with Pierre Salinger
ABOVE HAWAII
ABOVE WASHINGTON(D.C.)
ABOVE NEW YORK with George Plimpton and Paul Goldberger

Softcover, ninety-six full color pages, 9 x 12 inches.

ABOVE MACKINAC with Phil Porter
ABOVE CARMEL, MONTEREY AND BIG SUR
    with Harold Gilliam

Available from Cameron and Company and at fine Booksellers